dhammapada

dhammapada

THE WAY OF TRUTH

Translated from the Pāli by
Sangharakshita

Published by
Windhorse Publications
38 Newmarket Road
Cambridge
CB5 8DT

info@windhorsepublications.com
windhorsepublications.com

© Sangharakshita 2001
Second paperback edition 2008,
reprinted 2011, 2014, 2016, 2022

Printed and bound by
Bell & Bain Ltd,
Glasgow, UK

Cover design Vincent Stokes

British Library Cataloguing in Publication Data:
A catalogue record for this book is available
from the British Library.

ISBN: 978 1 899579 93 8

Cover illustration The Buddha (1906)
Odilon Redon (1840-1916)
Louvre, D.A.G. (fonds Orsay)
© photo RMN – Jean Schorman

CONTENTS

About the Translator   vii

Preface   1

I   Pairs   13

II   Mindfulness   18

III   The Mind   22

IV   Flowers   25

V   The Spiritually Immature   29

VI   The Spiritually Mature   34

VII   The (Supremely) Worthy   38

VIII   The Thousands   42

IX   Evil   47

X   Punishment   51

XI   Decay   56

XII   Self   59

XIII The World 62

XIV The Enlightened One 66

XV Happiness 71

XVI Affections 75

XVII Anger 79

XVIII Stains 83

XIX The Man of Principle 89

XX The Way 94

XXI The Miscellaneous 99

XXII The Woeful State 104

XXIII The Elephant 108

XXIV Craving 112

XXV The Almsman 120

XXVI The Brāhmaṇa 126

Notes 139

Glossary 143

Further Reading 147

About the Translator

Sangharakshita was born Dennis Lingwood in South London, in 1925. Largely self-educated, he developed an interest in the cultures and philosophies of the East early on, and realized that he was a Buddhist at the age of sixteen.

The Second World War took him, as a conscript, to India, where he stayed on to become the Buddhist monk Sangharakshita. After studying for some years under leading teachers from the major Buddhist traditions, he went on to teach and write extensively. He also played a key part in the revival of Buddhism in India, particularly through his work among followers of Dr B.R. Ambedkar.

After twenty years in India, he returned to England to establish the Friends of the Western Buddhist Order (FWBO) in 1967, and the Western Buddhist Order (called Trailokya Bauddha Mahasangha in India) in 1968. A translator between East and West, between the traditional world and the modern, between principles and practices, Sangharakshita brought to the task a depth of experience and clarity of thought that have been appreciated throughout the world. He always particularly emphasized the decisive significance of commitment in the spiritual life, the paramount value of spiritual friendship and community, the link between religion and art, and the need for a 'new society' supportive of spiritual aspirations and ideals.

The FWBO was renamed the Triratna Buddhist Community in 2010 and is now an international Buddhist movement with over sixty centres on five continents. The last five years of Sangharakshita's life were happily spent at Adhisthana in rural Herefordshire, UK – a retreat centre and the headquarters of the Triratna Buddhist Order. He died in October 2018 and is buried at Adhisthana.

PREFACE

THE BUDDHA was born towards the end of the fifth century BCE, renounced the world at the age of twenty-nine, attained Enlightenment six years later, and spent the remaining forty-five years of his life communicating the Truth he had discovered to anyone who was willing to learn.

He communicated that Truth orally, by means of the spoken word, though many people were also deeply moved by his mere presence. His words made a deep impression on his hearers, so that some of them remembered them all their lives and both before and after his death repeated them for the benefit of others. In this way there sprang up and developed an *oral tradition*, which not only preserved the Buddha's teaching but organized, edited, and amplified it in various ways. The process of oral transmission lasted for several hundred years and probably it was not until the first century BCE that the Buddha's discourses and sayings began to be committed to writing.

By this time that tradition had become very rich, the more especially as it now included exegetical and commentarial material by several successive generations of the Buddha's followers. By this time, too, those followers had become divided into a number of different schools, each of which transmitted, in its own language, its own particular version of orally transmitted material. When the oral tradition of the Buddha's teaching came finally to be written down, therefore, it was written down in at least four different languages or dialects, one of them being the language now known as Pāli.

This Pāli version of the oral tradition, which was committed to writing in Sri Lanka in the first century BCE by members of the Theravāda School, is the only version of that material to have survived complete in the original language, and as such it is of enormous historical and spiritual importance. It is divided into three *piṭakas* or 'baskets', a basket of monastic rules, a basket of discourses, and a basket of further teaching, the last being actually the work of latter-day followers. The basket of discourses or Sutta Piṭaka is divided into five collections, the fifth of which is the *Khuddaka-Nikāya* or 'Little Collection'. The 'Little Collection' consists of fifteen separate works, some very long and some quite short. The *Dhammapada* is one of these.

Though none of the other literary versions of the oral tradition has survived complete in the original language, a handful of separate works, or portions of works, fortunately are still available to us. Thus in addition to the Pāli *Dhamma-pada* we have a Prakrit *Dhamapada* and a Sanskrit *Dharma-pada* (also known as the *Udānavarga*). The Chinese Buddhist Canon also contains four texts of this name, all translated from different Sanskrit originals. Such comparative studies as have so far been made reveal no basic discrepancies among the various recensions of the work, whether Pāli, Prakrit, or Sanskrit. As I have written elsewhere, 'All consist of the same type of material organized in the same way, that is to say, of verses embodying ethical and spiritual precepts grouped more or less according to subject under various sectional headings. Though the total number of verses is not the same, and though the selection of verses, as well as the number and nature of the sections into which they are classified, differ considerably from one text to another, all the *Dhammapada-s* have certain blocks of verses in common. Some of these blocks are found elsewhere in the Sūtra Piṭaka; others appear to be peculiar to the *Dhammapada* liter-ature. It would seem, therefore, that taking these blocks, which together constituted the basic text,... each of the early schools composed a *Dhammapada* of its own.'

That the Pāli *Dhammapada* is at present the best known of this class of Buddhist canonical texts is largely the result of historical accident. Since its appearance in a Latin version in 1855 it has been repeatedly translated into the principal European and Asian languages, 'the depth and universality of its doctrine, the purity and earnestness of its moral teach-ing, and the sublimity of its spiritual ideal, combined with

the refined simplicity and pellucid poetical beauty of its
language, winning for it an honoured place in world
literature.' Small wonder, then, that the *Dhammapada*
should now be one of the best known and best loved of all
Buddhist scriptures, or that for many Western Buddhists, ir-
respective of school, it should be a perpetual source of
inspiration.

For me it has been a source of inspiration, encouragement,
and guidance for well over fifty years. Indeed, I sometimes
think that the *Dhammapada* contains, at least in principle, as
much of the Buddha's teaching as most of us really need to
know in order to progress towards Enlightenment. As the
Buddha himself tells us in verse 100, 'Better than a thousand
meaningless words collected together (in the Vedic oral tradition) is a single meaningful word on hearing which one
becomes tranquil.' There are many such meaningful words
in the *Dhammapada* – words that are of infinitely greater
value than the tens of thousands of meaningless words we
hear every day of our lives.

Four episodes in the history of my relationship with the
Dhammapada stand out with particular vividness.

The first occurred in 1944. I had just arrived in Delhi, and
being already a Buddhist went looking for a Buddhist tem-
ple. Eventually I found one, the first I had ever seen. Inside
the entrance there was a bookstall, and among the books I
bought that day was an English translation of the *Dhammapada* complete with the Pāli text in Devanagari script.
Thereafter the orange-covered pocket volume accompanied

me to Sri Lanka, to Singapore, and then back to India, where it was the constant companion of my years as a freelance wandering ascetic.

It is to those years of wandering that the next episode belongs. I was staying at a Hindu ashram in North Malabar, and during my stay devoted the period of my morning walk to learning the *Dhammapada* by heart in the original Pāli, reciting the verses out loud as I strode along the road. As I knew no Pāli, though I had learned the Devanagari script while in Sri Lanka, I had to recite the verses parrot-fashion with only a general idea of their meaning. At that time I was a great believer in the value of learning scriptures and poetry by heart, as I still am today.

The third episode in the history of my relationship with the *Dhammapada* finds me living in Benares with the venerable Jagdish Kashyap, my first teacher, with whom I studied Pāli, Abhidharma, and Logic. One of the texts I studied with him was the *Dhammapada*. Though I never became a Pāli scholar, as Kashyap-ji perhaps hoped I might, I at least managed to acquire from him a knowledge of the language sufficient to enable me, many years later, to attempt a *Dhammapada* translation of my own.

The last of these episodes took place in Poona, not long before my return to the West in 1964. In 1956 hundreds of thousands of Hindus who had beentreated as Untouchables by members of the higher castes converted to Buddhism, and since then I had spent much of my time travelling from place to place throughout Central and Western India teaching them the fundamentals of the Dharma. On one of my visits to Poona I conducted a four-week training course in Buddhism, in the context of which I gave a running commentary on all twenty-six chapters of the *Dhammapada*. Few, if any, of the participants had encountered the *Dhammapada* before, and I was deeply moved to see the effect the inspired words of the Buddha had on them all, including the uneducated and even illiterate. They could well have exclaimed, as did so many in the Buddha's own day, that it was as though what was overthrown was raised up, or what was hidden revealed, or the way pointed out to him that wandered astray, or a light held up in the darkness so that those that had eyes might see.

During the seventies and eighties, back in England, I led seminars on different chapters of the *Dhammapada*, though without ever covering the entire work as I had done in Poona. It was at this time, and in connection with those seminars, that I started translating the *Dhammapada* and got about a third of the way through the text. Circumstances then obliged me to put the work aside for a while, and as in the interval several new translations of the *Dhammapada* had appeared I eventually concluded there was no need for me to finish mine. Copies of the chapters I had translated did, however, circulate in duplicated form among friends and disciples, many of whom assured me that they found my version of these chapters more useful than any other. They also urged me to finish the work of translating the remaining chapters and in the end I promised to do so. This promise I redeemed last year, here in the peace and solitude of the green valley that is Guhyaloka, and in this way, totally immersed as I was in the inspired words of the Buddha, spent one of the happiest months of my life.

There have been more than thirty English translations of the *Dhammapada* or Way of Truth, or Footfalls of the Law, or Statement of Principles, as the work has been variously called, and it might have been thought that notwithstanding the urgings of friends and disciples another one was hardly necessary. But of a text like the *Dhammapada* there cannot be too many translations, not only because the more translations there are the more widely the work is likely to be known but because no single translation can fully exhaust the meaning of the original. In this present version I have striven not only to be accurate but, in particular, to reproduce the directness and sense of urgency I detect in many of the verses – a directness and sense of urgency which most other translations entirely fail to capture. At times, indeed, it is as though the Buddha is speaking personally to us across the centuries, reminding us of our faults, encouraging us to persevere, and pointing out the ultimate Goal. For this reason I have not burdened the translation with a commentary, so that to the extent that the exigencies of translation permit there should be nothing to stand between the reader and the Buddha.

A few words about the way in which I have translated certain key terms may not be out of place.

Originally I had rendered the word *arahant* as 'the New Man', but since then the expression has been so seriously devalued that I have had to drop it. Instead, I have translated *arahant*, more literally, as 'the (Supremely) Worthy One', the bracketed adverb and initial capitals indicating that inasmuch as an Arahant is one who has attained Nirvāṇa or Enlightenment, he (or she) is 'worthy' in the highest possible sense. The term *bhikkhu* is often translated 'monk', but this rendering I have avoided, partly because the word 'monk' is so overlaid with Christian connotations as to be quite misleading when used in a Buddhist context and partly because of the confusion that has been created by the appearance, in recent years, of Zen 'married monks' of both sexes. The literal meaning of *bhikkhu* is one who lives on alms, and I have therefore translated it as 'almsman'. Though *brāhmaṇa* is a multivalent term, and as such difficult to translate by any one word, its meaning within the context of the *Dhammapada* is reasonably clear, and I have therefore left it untranslated, except that in the few instances where it refers to a member of the Vedic priestly caste I have given it in its anglicized form. The term *samaṇa*, literally 'one who strives (spiritually)', is quite accurately rendered by 'ascetic', which is the usual translation, but in order to emphasize the latter's ultimate derivation from the Greek *askeīn*, 'to exercise', and to dissociate it from any suggestion of self-mortification, I have spelt the word with a 'k' instead of with a 'c'.

The terms *bāla* and *paṇḍita* designate two contrasting types of persons – 'the fool' and 'the wise', as they are usually translated. *Bāla*, however, means not so much a fool as one who is childish, lacking in moral sense. I have therefore translated *bāla* as 'the (spiritually) immature person' and *paṇḍita*, accordingly, as 'the (spiritually) mature person'. *Dhammaṭṭha* has been rendered as 'the man of principle' rather than as 'the righteous' in order to avoid the latter word's rather biblical overtones.

Now that it is at last finished, this latest translation of the *Dhammapada* goes forth from the secluded, peaceful valley where most of the work on it has been done into a world which is far from peaceful. It goes forth, in particular, into a Western world increasingly dominated by the forces of greed, as represented by consumerism, hatred, as represented by ruthless economic competition, and delusion, as represented by a variety of ideologies from scientism to religious fundamentalism. Thus it goes forth into a world greatly in need of the qualities of simplicity, contentment, kindness, gentleness, serenity, and self-control inculcated by the Buddha in the *Dhammapada* – qualities that lead, in the long run, to the enjoyment of that vision of the Truth which alone can satisfy the deepest longings of the human heart. May this present translation play a part in making those qualities more widespread and more active among us.

Sangharakshita

Guhyaloka
Spain
31 July 2000

DHAMMAPADA

I

PAIRS

1

1 Experiences are preceded by mind, led by mind, and produced by mind. If one speaks or acts with an impure mind, suffering follows even as the cart-wheel follows the hoof of the ox (drawing the cart).

2

2 Experiences are preceded by mind, led by mind, and produced by mind. If one speaks or acts with a pure mind, happiness follows like a shadow that never departs.

3

3   Those who entertain such thoughts as 'He abused me, he beat me, he conquered me, he robbed me,' will not still their hatred.

4

4   Those who do not entertain such thoughts as 'He abused me, he beat me, he conquered me, he robbed me,' will still their hatred.

5

5   Not by hatred are hatreds ever pacified here (in the world). They are pacified by love. This is the eternal law.

6

6   Others do not realize that we are all heading for death. Those who do realize it will compose their quarrels.

7

7   As the wind blows down a weak tree, so Māra[1] overthrows one who lives seeing the (unlovely as) lovely, whose senses are uncontrolled, who is immoderate in food, lazy, and of inferior vigour.

8

8 As the wind does not blow down the rocky
mountain peak, so Māra does not overthrow one
who lives seeing the (unlovely as) unlovely, whose
senses are controlled, who is moderate in food, and
whose faith and vigour are aroused.

9

9 He is not worthy of the yellow robe who takes it
(while still) not free from impurity, and lacking in
self-restraint and truth.

10

10 He is worthy of the yellow robe who has made
an end to all impurity, who is well established in
virtuous conduct (*sīla*), and who is endowed with
self-restraint and truth.

11

11 Those who take the unreal for the real, and who
in the real see the unreal, they, wandering in the
sphere of wrong thought, will not attain the real.

12

12 Those who have known the real as the real,

and the unreal as the unreal, they, moving in the
sphere of right thought, will attain the real.

13

13 As the rain penetrates the badly thatched house,
so lust enters the (spiritually) undeveloped mind.

14

14 As the rain does not penetrate into the well-
thatched house, so lust does not enter the
(spiritually) well-developed mind.

15

15 The evildoer grieves in both worlds; he grieves
'here' and he grieves 'there'.[2] He suffers and
torments himself seeing his own foul deeds.

16

16 The doer of good rejoices in both (worlds); he
rejoices 'here' and he rejoices 'there'. He rejoices
and is glad seeing his own pure deeds.

17

17 The evildoer burns in both (worlds); he burns
'here' and he burns 'there'. He burns (with remorse)

thinking he has done evil, and he burns (with suffering) having gone (after death) to an evil state.

18

18 The doer of good delights in both (worlds); he delights 'here' and he delights 'there'. He delights (in this life) thinking he has done good and he delights (after death) having gone to a state of happiness.

19

19 He who for his own benefit constantly recites the (canonical) literature[3] but does not act accordingly, that heedless man, like a cowherd that counts the cows of others, is not enriched by the asketic life.

20

20 He who for his own benefit recites even a little of the (canonical) literature but lives in accordance with its principles, abandoning craving, hatred, and delusion, possessed of right knowledge, with mind well freed, clinging to nothing in this or any other world, *he* is enriched by the asketic life.

II

MINDFULNESS

1

21 Mindfulness is the Way to the Immortal,[4] unmindfulness the way to death. Those who are mindful do not die, (whereas) the unmindful are like the dead.

2

22 Knowing the distinction of mindfulness the spiritually mature (*paṇḍita-s*) rejoice in mindfulness and take delight in the sphere of the Noble Ones (*ariya-s*).

3

23 Absorbed in superconscious states (*jhāna-s*), recollected, and ever exerting themselves, those wise ones (*dhīra-s*) realize Nirvāṇa, the unsurpassed security.

4

24 Whoever is energetic, recollected, pure in conduct, considerate, self-restrained, of righteous life, and mindful, the glory of such a one waxes exceedingly.

5

25 By means of energy, mindfulness, self-restraint, and control, let the man of understanding (*medhāvī*) make (for himself) an island that no flood can overwhelm.

6

26 Out of their evil understanding the spiritually immature (*bāla-s*) abandon themselves to unmindfulness. The man of understanding guards mindfulness as his chief treasure.

7

27 Do not abandon yourselves to unmindfulness;
have no intimacy with sensuous delights. The
mindful person, absorbed in superconscious states,
gains ample bliss.

8

28 As a dweller in the mountains looks down on
those who live in the valley, so the spiritually mature
person, the hero free from sorrow, having driven out
unmindfulness by means of mindfulness, ascends to
the Palace of Wisdom and looks down at the
sorrowful, spiritually immature multitude (below).

9

29 Mindful among the unmindful, wide awake
among the sleeping, the man of good understanding
forges ahead like a swift horse outdistancing a feeble
hack.

10

30 By means of mindfulness, Maghava (i.e., Indra)
attained to the chieftaincy of the gods. Mindfulness
is always praised, unmindfulness always despised.

11

31 The almsman (*bhikkhu*) who delights in mindfulness (and) who regards unmindfulness with fear advances like fire, burning up fetters gross and subtle.

12

32 The almsman who delights in mindfulness (and) who regards unmindfulness with fear is not liable to regression. He is in the presence of Nirvāṇa.

III

THE MIND

1

33 As a fletcher straightens the arrow, so the man of understanding makes straight the trembling unsteady mind, which is difficult to guard (and) difficult to restrain.

2

34 As a fish threshes from side to side when taken from one abode to another and cast on dry land, so the mind throbs and vibrates (with the strain) as it abandons the domain of Māra.

3

35 (The mind) is frivolous and difficult to control,
alighting on whatever it pleases. It is good to tame
the mind. A tamed mind brings happiness.

4

36 The mind is extremely subtle and difficult to
grasp, alighting on whatever it pleases. Let the man
of understanding keep watch over the mind. A
guarded mind brings happiness.

5

37 Far-ranging and lone-faring is the mind,
incorporeal and abiding in the cave (of the heart).
Those who bring it under control are freed from the
bonds of Māra.

6

38 His wisdom does not attain to perfection whose
mind is unsettled, who is ignorant of the Real Truth
(*saddhamma*), and whose faith wavers.

7

39 There is no fear for someone who is awake,
whose mind is uncontaminated by craving, (and)

unperplexed, (and) who has given up vice and
virtue.

8

40 Perceiving the body to be (fragile) like a clay pot,
(and) fortifying the mind as though it were a city,
with the sword of wisdom make war on Māra. Free
from attachment, keep watch over what has been
won.

9

41 Before long, this body, devoid of consciousness,
will lie rejected on the ground like a useless faggot.

10

42 Whatever foe may do to foe, or hater to hater,
greater is the harm done (to oneself) by a wrongly
directed mind.

11

43 Neither mother nor father, nor any other
relative, can do one as much good as a perfectly
directed mind.

IV

FLOWERS

1

44 Who shall conquer the earth and the Realm of Death with its deities? Who shall make out the well-taught Verses of Truth as an expert picks flowers?

2

45 The Learner (of the Transcendental Path) shall conquer the Realm of Death with its deities. The Learner shall make out the well-taught Verses of Truth as an expert picks flowers.

3

46 Seeing the body as froth, (and) thoroughly comprehending its mirage-nature, let one proceed unseen by the King of Death, having broken the flower-tipped arrows[5] of Māra.

4

47 As a great flood carries away a sleeping village, so death bears off the man who, possessed of longing, plucks only the flowers (of existence).

5

48 The Destroyer brings under his sway the man who, possessed by longing, plucks only the flowers (of existence), (and) who is insatiable in sexual passions.

6

49 Let the silent sage move about in the village as the bee goes taking honey from the flower without harming colour or fragrance.

7

50 One should pay no heed to the faults of others, what they have done and not done. Rather should

one consider the things that one has oneself done
and not done.

8

51 Like a beautiful flower, brightly coloured but
without scent, even so useless is the well-uttered
speech of one who does not act accordingly.

9

52 Like a beautiful flower, brightly coloured and
scented, even so useful is the well-uttered speech of
one who acts accordingly.

10

53 As many garlands are made from a heap of
flowers, so one who is a mortal born should perform
many ethically skilful deeds.

11

54 The fragrance of flowers, of sandalwood, of
aromatic resin or jasmine, does not go against the
wind, (whereas) the fragrance of the good does go
against the wind.

12

55 Sandalwood or aromatic resin, blue lotus, or
wild jasmine, of all these kinds of fragrance, the
odour of virtue is unsurpassed.

13

56 Insignificant in comparison is this fragrance of
aromatic resin and sandalwood. The fragrance of
virtue it is that blows among the gods as the highest.

14

57 Māra does not find the path of those who are
virtuous, who live mindfully, and who are freed
through Perfect Knowledge (*sammadaññā*).

15

58 As pink lotuses, sweet-scented and lovely, spring
from a heap of rubbish thrown in the highway,

16

59 so among those who have become (as) rubbish,
(among) ignorant, ordinary people, the Disciple of
the Perfectly Enlightened One shines forth
exceedingly in wisdom.

V

THE SPIRITUALLY IMMATURE

1

60 Long is the night to the wakeful, long the league to one who is exhausted (with travel). Long is the process of faring (through repeated existences) to those spiritually immature ones who do not know the real truth (*saddhamma*).

2

61 If he who goes about (in search of truth) does not find one better than or (at least) similar to himself, let him firmly lead a solitary life. There is no companionship (for him) with the spiritually immature.

3

62 The spiritually immature person vexes himself (thinking) 'Sons are mine, riches are mine'. He himself is not his own, even; how then sons? how then riches?

4

63 The spiritually immature person who recognizes his immaturity is to that extent mature; the spiritually immature one who thinks of himself as mature is termed immature indeed.

5

64 Though throughout his life a spiritually immature person attends upon (or: honours) one who is spiritually mature, he does not necessarily know the truth, any more than the spoon knows the taste of the soup.

6

65 If for a moment a wise man attends upon one who is spiritually mature, he quickly perceives the truth, as the tongue at once detects the taste of the soup.

7

66 Of evil understanding, the spiritually immature
live as enemies to themselves, committing sinful
deeds, the consequences of which are bitter.

8

67 That deed is not well done which, being done,
one repents, (and) the result of which one suffers
with tearful face and lamentations.

9

68 That deed is well done which, being done, one
does not repent, (and) the result of which one
receives gladly.

10

69 So long as it has not ripened, the spiritually
immature one thinks sin as sweet as honey; (but)
when sin does ripen, then the spiritually immature
one suffers a downfall.

11

70 Month after month, a spiritually immature
person may eat his food with the tip of a blade of
(sacred) kusa-grass,[6] (yet) his worth is not a fraction

(lit., not a sixteenth part) of those who have
ascertained the truth.

12

71 Unlike milk, which curdles immediately, the sin
that has been committed does not at once bear fruit.
(Instead) it pursues the spiritually immature person
like a fire covered with ashes, burning him (only
after a time).

13

72 The spiritually immature person wins
(theoretical religious) knowledge only to his own
disadvantage; it destroys his better nature while
splitting his head.

14

73 One who is spiritually immature desires a false
reputation, honour among fellow almsmen,
authority over monastic settlements, and respect
from the families (living) round about.

15

74 'Let both those householders and those who
have gone forth (from the household life) approve
what I have done; let them be subject to me in all

undertakings, great and small.' Such is the wish of
the spiritually immature, (as a result of which) his
craving and conceit increase.

16

75 One thing is that which leads to (worldly) gain;
quite another the way that leads to Nirvāṇa. Thus
comprehending, let the almsman, the disciple of the
Buddha, take no delight in respectful greetings, but
devote himself to solitude.

VI

THE SPIRITUALLY MATURE

1

76 Should one see a man of understanding who, as if indicating a (buried) treasure, points out faults and administers reproof, let one associate with such a spiritually mature person. To associate with one like this is good, not evil.

2

77 Let him instruct, let him advise, let him restrain (one) from uncivilized behaviour, (and the result will be that) he will be dear to the good and detestable to the bad.

3

78 Do not associate with evil friends; do not associate with low fellows. Associate with spiritual friends; associate with superior men (*purisuttama-s*).

4

79 One who has imbibed the Truth lives happily with well-seeing mind. The spiritually mature person delights in the Truth made known by the Noble (*ariya-s*).

5

80 Irrigators draw off waters; fletchers straighten arrows; carpenters shape wood; the spiritually mature discipline themselves.

6

81 As a solid rock cannot be shaken by the wind, so the spiritually mature person is unmoved by praise or blame.

7

82 Hearing the teachings (of the Buddha) the spiritually mature become clear (or calm) like a deep lake (suddenly) becoming clear or undisturbed.

8

83 True men give up everything; the righteous do not speak wishing for sensuous pleasures. Touched now by pleasure, now by pain, the spiritually mature show neither elation nor depression.

9

84 Not for one's own sake, nor for the sake of others, should one desire sons, wealth, or territory; one should not desire success for oneself by unrighteous means. He (who behaves in such a way) is virtuous, is wise, is righteous.

10

85 Few among men are those who go to the Further Shore. The other (ordinary) people chase up and down this shore.

11

86 Those people who conform themselves to the well-explained Truth of Things and who are desirous of (reaching) the Further Shore will pass over the Realm of Death, so difficult to transcend.

12

87 Forsaking dark ways, the spiritually mature
person cultivates the bright. Coming from home to
the homeless (life), he (abides) in solitude (which)
is hard to enjoy.

13

88 Giving up delight in sensuous pleasures the
spiritually mature person, the man-of-no-
possessions, should purify himself from (all) mental
defilements.

14

89 They whose minds have cultivated to perfection
the Factors of Enlightenment[7] and who, free from
clinging, delight in the giving up of attachment,
those bias-free radiant ones become Cool (*nibbutā*)
even in this world (i.e., in this life).

VII

THE (SUPREMELY) WORTHY

1

90   The burning fever of passion does not exist for one who has finished his journey (i.e., completed his spiritual evolution), who is free from sorrow, wholly emancipated, and released from all the bonds (of conditionality).

2

91   The mindful who leave home do not delight in an abode; like wild geese quitting a lake, they abandon whatever security they have.

3

92 Those who do not accumulate (material or mental possessions), who thoroughly understand (the true nature of) the food they eat, and whose range of experience (lit., pasture) is liberation through (the realization of) the Empty (*suñña*) and Unconditioned (*animitta*), their path, like that of birds in the sky, is difficult to trace.

4

93 He whose impurities are extinct, who is not attached to food, and whose range of experience (lit., pasture) is liberation through (the realization of) the Empty (*suñña*) and Unconditioned (*animitta*), his path, like that of birds in the sky, is difficult to trace.

5

94 He whose senses are pacified like horses well controlled by the charioteer, who has eradicated conceit and who is free from impurities – the very gods love a man of such (good) qualities (as these).

6

95 Like the earth, he offers no opposition; like the main pillar (of the city gate), he stands firm. He is

(pure) like a lake free from mud. For a man of such (good) qualities (as these) there are no more wanderings (from life to life).

7

96 Tranquil is the thought, tranquil the word and deed, of that supremely tranquil person who is emancipated through Perfect Knowledge.

8

97 He is a superior man (*uttamaporiso*) who does not (merely) believe (but) who knows the Unmade, who has severed all links (with conditioned existence), put an end to the occasions (of good and evil), and who has renounced (lit., vomited up) all worldly hopes.

9

98 Whether village or forest, plain or hill, delightful is that spot where the (Supremely) Worthy dwell.

10

99 Delightful are the forests where ordinary people find no pleasure. Those who are free from passion

delight (in them), (for) they do not go in quest of sensuous enjoyment.

VIII

THE THOUSANDS

1

100 Better than a thousand meaningless words collected together (in the Vedic oral tradition) is a single meaningful word on hearing which one becomes tranquil.

2

101 Better than a thousand meaningless verses collected together (in the Vedic oral tradition) is one (meaningful) line of verse on hearing which one becomes tranquil.

3

102   Though one should recite a hundred (Vedic)
verses, (verses) without meaning, better is one line
(or: a single word) of Dhamma on hearing which
one becomes tranquil.

4

103   Though one should conquer in battle
thousands upon thousands of men, yet he who
conquers himself is (truly) the greatest in battle.

5

104   It is indeed better to conquer oneself than to
conquer other people. Of a man who has subdued
himself, (and) who lives (self-)controlled,

6

105   neither a god nor a celestial musician
(*gandhabba*), nor Māra together with Brahmā, can
undo the victory – the victory of a person who is
(subdued and controlled) like that.

7

106   If month after month for a hundred years one
should offer sacrifices by the thousand, and if for a
single moment one should venerate a (spiritually)

developed person, better is that (act of) veneration than the hundred years (of sacrifices).

8

107 Though one should tend the sacred fire in the forest for a hundred years, yet if he venerates a (spiritually) developed person even for a moment, better is that (act of) veneration than the hundred years (spent tending the sacred fire).

9

108 Whatever oblations and sacrifices one might offer here on earth in the course of the whole (Vedic) religious year, seeking to gain merit thereby, all that is not a quarter (as meritorious) as paying respect to those who live uprightly, which is (indeed) excellent.

10

109 For him who is of a reverential disposition, constantly respecting his elders, four things constantly increase: life, beauty, happiness and strength.

II

110 Though one should live a hundred years
unethical and unintegrated (*asamāhita*), better is one
single day lived ethically and absorbed (in higher
meditative states).

12

111 Though one should live a hundred years of evil
understanding and unintegrated, better is one single
day lived possessed of wisdom and absorbed (in
higher meditative states).

13

112 Better than a hundred years lived lazily and
with inferior energy is one single day lived with
energy aroused and fortified.

14

113 Better than a hundred years lived unaware of
the rise and fall (of conditioned things) is one single
day lived aware of the rise and fall (of conditioned
things).

15

114 Better than a hundred years lived unaware of the Deathless State is one single day lived aware of the Deathless State.

16

115 Better than a hundred years lived unaware of the Supreme Truth *(dhammam uttamaṃ)* is one single day lived aware of the Supreme Truth.

IX

EVIL

1

116 Be quick to do what is (morally) beautiful.
Restrain the mind from evil. He who is sluggish in
doing good, his mind delights in evil.

2

117 Should a man (once) do evil, let him not make a
habit of it; let him not set his heart on it. Painful is
the heaping up of evil.

3

118 Should a man (once) do good, let him make a habit of it; let him set his heart on it. Happy is the heaping up of good.

4

119 As long as it bears no fruit, so long the evildoer sees the evil (he has done) as good. When it bears fruit (in the form of suffering) he recognizes it as evil.

5

120 As long as it bears no fruit, so long the good man sees (the good he has done) as evil. When it bears fruit (in the form of happiness), then he recognizes it as good.

6

121 Do not underestimate evil, (thinking) 'It will not approach me.' A water-pot becomes full by the (constant) falling of drops of water. (Similarly) the spiritually immature person little by little fills himself with evil.

7

122 Do not underestimate good, (thinking) 'It will not approach me.' A water-pot becomes full by the (constant) falling of drops of water. (Similarly) the wise man little by little fills himself with good.

8

123 As a merchant (travelling) with a small caravan and much wealth avoids a dangerous road, or as one desirous of life shuns poison, so should one keep clear of evil.

9

124 If one has no wound in one's hand one may (safely) handle poison. The unwounded hand is not affected by poison. (Similarly) no evil befalls him who does no wrong.

10

125 Whoever offends against an innocent man, one who is pure and faultless, to that spiritually immature person the evil (he has committed) comes back like fine dust thrown against the wind.

II

126 Some (beings) arise (by way of conception) in the womb. Evildoers are born in a state of woe. Those who do good go to heaven. Those who are free from defilements become utterly 'Cool'.

12

127 Not in the sky, nor in the midst of the sea, nor yet in the clefts of the mountains, nowhere in the world (in fact) is there any place to be found where, having entered, one can abide free from (the consequences of) one's evil deeds.

13

128 Not in the sky, nor in the midst of the sea, nor yet in the clefts of mountains, nowhere in the world (in fact) is there any place to be found where, having entered, one will not be overcome by death.

X

PUNISHMENT

1

129 All (living beings) are terrified of punishment (*daṇḍa*); all fear death. Making comparison (of others) with oneself, one should neither kill nor cause to kill.

2

130 All (living beings) are terrified of punishment (*daṇḍa*); to all, life is dear. Making comparison (of others) with oneself, one should neither kill nor cause to kill.

3

131 Whoever torments with the stick (*daṇḍa*) creatures desirous of happiness, he himself thereafter, seeking happiness, will not obtain happiness.

4

132 Whoever does not torment with the stick (*daṇḍa*) creatures desirous of happiness, he himself thereafter, seeking happiness, will obtain happiness.

5

133 Do not speak roughly to anyone: those thus spoken to will answer back. Painful indeed is angry talk, (as a result of which) one will experience retribution.

6

134 If you (can) silence yourself like a shattered metal plate you have already attained Nirvāṇa: no anger is found in you.

7

135 As a cowherd drives cows out to pasture with a stick, so do old age and death drive the life out of living beings.

8

136 A spiritually immature person performs evil deeds not realizing (their true nature). By his own actions is the man of evil understanding tormented (lit., burned) as though consumed by fire.

9

137 Whoever inflicts punishment on the innocent, (or) who offends against the unoffending, he speedily falls into one of the ten states:

10

138 He meets either with intense physical pain, or material loss, or bodily injury, or serious illness, or mental derangement;

11

139 Or (he meets with) trouble from the Government or a serious accusation, or bereavement, or loss of wealth:

12

140 Or else his houses are consumed by fire, (while) on the dissolution of the body that man of evil understanding is reborn in a state of woe.

13

141 Not going about naked, not (the wearing of) matted locks, not abstention from food, not sleeping on the (bare) ground, not (smearing the body with) dust and ashes, nor yet (the practice of) squatting (on the balls of the feet), can purify a mortal who has not overcome his doubts.

14

142 If one who is richly adorned lives in tranquillity, is calm, controlled, assured (of eventual enlightenment), and devotes himself to the spiritual life, laying down the stick with regard to all living beings, then (despite his being richly adorned), he is a brāhmaṇa, he is an asketic, he is an almsman.

15

143 In the (whole) world is there a man to be found who, restrained by a sense of shame, avoids censure as a good horse avoids the whip?

16

144 Like a good horse touched by the whip, be zealous and stirred by profound religious emotion. By means of faith, upright conduct, energy, concentration (*samādhi*), and investigation of the

Truth, (as well as by being) endowed with (spiritual) knowledge and (righteous) behaviour, and by being mindful, leave this great suffering behind.

17

145 Irrigators draw off the waters; fletchers straighten arrows; carpenters shape wood; righteous men discipline themselves.

XI

DECAY

1

146 What mirth can there be, what pleasure, when all the time (everything) is blazing (with the threefold fire of suffering, impermanence, and insubstantiality)? Covered (though you are) in blind darkness, you do not seek a light!

2

147 Look at this painted doll (i.e., the body), this pretentious mass of sores, wretched and full of cravings (or: much hankered after), nothing of which is stable or lasting!

3

148 Wasted away is this body, a nest of disease, and perishable. The putrid mass breaks up: death is the end of life.

4

149 When like gourds in autumn these dove-grey bones lie here discarded, what pleasure (can one take) in looking at them?

5

150 (The body) is a city built of bones and plastered with flesh and blood, (a city) wherein lie concealed decay and death, pride and hypocrisy.

6

151 Even the richly decorated royal chariots (in time) wear out; likewise the body also perishes. (But) the Truth (*dhamma*) of the good does not perish, (for) those who are good indeed speak of it to the good.

7

152 The man of little learning lives like a stalled ox: his flesh increases but his wisdom does not.

8

153 Many a birth have I undergone in this (process of) faring on (in the round of conditioned existence), seeking the builder of the house and not finding him. Painful is (such) repeated birth.

9

154 House-builder, (now) you are seen! Never again shall you build (me) a house. Your rafters are all broken, your ridgepole shattered. The (conditioned) mind too has gone to destruction: one has attained to the cessation of craving.[8]

10

155 Those who have not led the spiritual life (*brahmacariya*), or obtained the wealth (of merit) in their youth, (such as these) brood over the past like aged herons in a pond without fish.

11

156 Those who have not led the spiritual life (*brahmacariya*), or obtained the wealth (of merit) in their youth, (such as these) lie like worn-out arrows, lamenting the things of old.

XII

SELF

I

157 If a man (really) regards himself as dear, let him well and truly protect himself. During one or another of the three watches (of the night) the spiritually mature person should keep wide awake.

2

158 First establish yourself in what is suitable, then advise others. The spiritually mature person should not besmirch himself (by acting otherwise).

3

159 Should you act as you advise others to act, then it would be (a case of) one who was (self-) controlled exercising control (over others). The self is truly difficult to control.

4

160 One is indeed one's own saviour (or: protector). What other saviour should there be? With oneself well-controlled, one finds a saviour (who is) hard to find.

5

161 The evil done by oneself, born of oneself, produced by oneself, destroys the man of evil understanding as a diamond pulverizes a piece of rock crystal.

6

162 He whose unprincipled behaviour is without limit, like a maluva(-creeper) overspreading a sal tree, does to his own self that which his enemy wishes (to do to him).

7

163 Easily done are things which are bad and not beneficial to oneself. What is (both) beneficial and good, that is exceedingly difficult to do.

8

164 The man of evil understanding who, on account of his (wrong) views, obstructs (or: rejects) the message of the (Supremely) Worthy, the noble ones, the men of authentic life, that wicked person, like a katthak(-reed), brings forth fruit (i.e., performs actions) to his own destruction.

9

165 A man besmirches himself by the evil he personally commits. (Similarly) he purifies himself by personally abstaining from evil. Purity and impurity are matters of personal experience: one man cannot purify another.

10

166 (Consequently) one should not neglect one's own (spiritual) welfare for the welfare of others, great as that may be. Clearly perceiving (what constitutes) one's personal welfare, one should devote oneself to one's own good.

XIII

THE WORLD

1

167 Don't follow inferior principles. Don't live heedlessly. Don't entertain false views. Don't be one who (by following inferior principles etc.) keeps the world going.

2

168 Get up! Don't be heedless! Live practising the Dhamma, (the Dhamma) which is good conduct. One who lives practising the Dhamma (*dhammacārī*) dwells happily (both) in this world and the other (world).

3

169 Live practising the Dhamma. Do not live behaving badly. One who lives practising the Dhamma (*dhammacārī*) dwells happily (both) in this world and the other (world).

4

170 Look upon (the world) as a bubble; look upon (it) as a mirage. The King of Death does not see one who looks upon the world in this way.

5

171 Come, (just) look at this world, which is like a decorated royal chariot in which the spiritually immature sink down (or: are dejected), but (with regard to which) there is no attachment on the part of those who really know.

6

172 One who having formerly been heedless later is not heedless, lights up the world like the moon (when) freed from clouds.

7

173 One who covers over the evil deeds he has done
with (ethically) skilful actions, lights up this world
like the moon (when) freed from clouds.

8

174 This world is (mentally) blinded; few see
clearly. Few are those who, like birds freed from the
net, go to heaven.

9

175 Swans fly on the path of the sun.[9] Those with
supernormal powers travel through the air. The
wise, having conquered Māra and his army, are led
(away) from the world.

10

176 There is no wrong that cannot be committed by
a lying person who has transgressed one (good)
principle (i.e., that of truthfulness), and who has
given up (all thought of) the other world.

11

177 Truly, misers do not get to the world of the
gods. (Only) the spiritually immature do not praise

giving. The wise man rejoices in giving, and therefore is happy in the hereafter.

12

178   The Fruit of Stream Entry is better than sole sovereignty over the earth, (better) than going to heaven, (better) than lordship over all the worlds.

XIV

THE ENLIGHTENED ONE

1

179 That Enlightened One whose sphere is endless, whose victory is irreversible, and after whose victory no (defilements) remain (to be conquered), by what track will you lead him (astray), the Trackless One?

2

180 That Enlightened One in whom there is not that ensnaring, entangling craving to lead anywhere (in conditioned existence), and whose sphere is endless, by what track will you lead him (astray), the Trackless One?

3

181   Those wise ones who are intent on absorption
(in higher meditative states) and who delight in the
calm of renunciation, even the gods love them,
those thoroughly enlightened and mindful ones.

4

182   Difficult is the attainment of the human state.
Difficult is the life of mortals. Difficult is the hearing
of the Real Truth (*saddhamma*). Difficult is the
appearance of the Enlightened Ones.

5

183   The not doing of anything evil, undertaking to
do what is (ethically) skilful (*kusala*), (and) complete
purification of the mind – this is the ordinance
(*sāsana*) of the Enlightened Ones.

6

184   Patient endurance is the best form of penance.
'Nirvāṇa is the Highest,' say the Enlightened Ones.
No (true) goer forth (from the household life) is he
who injures another, nor is he a true asketic who
persecutes others.

7

185 Not to speak evil, not to injure, to exercise restraint through the observance of the (almsman's) code of conduct, to be moderate in diet, to live alone, and to occupy oneself with higher mental states – this is the ordinance (sasana) of the Enlightened Ones.

8

186 Not (even) in a shower of money is satisfaction of desires to be found. 'Worldly pleasures are of little relish, (indeed) painful.' Thus understanding, the spiritually mature person

9

187 takes no delight even in heavenly pleasures. The disciple of the Fully, Perfectly Enlightened One takes delight (only) in the destruction of craving.

10

188 Many people, out of fear, flee for refuge to (sacred) hills, woods, groves, trees, and shrines.

11

189 In reality this is not a safe refuge. In reality this is not the best refuge. Fleeing to such a refuge one is not released from all suffering.

12

190 He who goes for refuge to the Enlightened One, to the Truth, and to the Spiritual Community, and who sees with perfect wisdom the Four Ariyan Truths –

13

191 namely, suffering, the origin of suffering, the passing beyond suffering, and the Ariyan Eightfold Way leading to the pacification of suffering –

14

192 (for him) this is a safe refuge, (for him) this is the best refuge. Having gone to such a refuge, one is released from all suffering.

15

193 Hard to come by is the Ideal Man (*purisājañña*). He is not born everywhere. Where such a wise one is born, that family grows happy.

16

194 Happy is the appearance of the Enlightened Ones. Happy is the teaching of the Real Truth (*saddhamma*). Happy is the unity of the Spiritual Community. Happy is the spiritual effort of the united.

17

195 He who reverences those worthy of reverence, whether Enlightened Ones or (their) disciples, (men) who have transcended illusion (*papañca*), and passed beyond grief and lamentation,

18

196 he who reverences those who are of such a nature, who (moreover) are at peace and without cause for fear, his merit is not to be reckoned as such and such.

XV

HAPPINESS

1

197 Happy indeed we live, friendly amid the haters.
Among men who hate we dwell free from hate.

2

198 Happy indeed we live, healthy amid the sick.
Among men who are sick we dwell free from
sickness.

3

199 Happy indeed we live, content amid the greedy.
Among men who are greedy we dwell free from
greed.

4

200 Happy indeed we live, we for whom there are no possessions (*kiñcana-s*). Feeders on rapture shall we be, like the gods of Brilliant Light.[10]

5

201 Victory begets hatred, (for) the defeated one experiences suffering. The tranquil one experiences happiness, giving up (both) victory and defeat.

6

202 There is no fire like lust, no blemish like demerit (*kali*), no suffering like the taking up of the (five) constituents (of conditioned existence), no happiness like peace.

7

203 Hunger is the worst disease, conditioned existence the worst suffering. Knowing this as it really is (one realizes that) Nirvāṇa is the highest happiness.

8

204 Health is the highest gain, contentment the greatest riches. The trustworthy are the best kinsmen, Nirvāṇa is the supreme happiness.

9

205 Having enjoyed the flavour of solitude and tranquillity, free from sorrow and free from sin, one enjoys the rapturous flavour of the Truth (*dhamma*).

10

206 Good it is to see the spiritually developed (*ariya-s*); to (actually) dwell with them is always happiness. By not seeing the spiritually immature, one indeed will be perpetually happy.

11

207 By living in company with the spiritually immature one grieves for a long time. Association with the spiritually immature is always painful, like association with an enemy. Association with the wise is pleasant, like the coming together of relatives.

12

208 (Therefore it is said:) Follow one who is wise, understanding, and learned, who bears the yoke of virtue, is religious and spiritually developed (*ariya*). Follow one of such a nature, as the moon follows the path of the stars.

XVI

AFFECTIONS

1

209 Devoting himself to the unbefitting and not devoting himself to the fitting, he, rejecting the (truly) good and grasping the (merely) pleasant, envies those who are devoted to the (truly) good.

2

210 Don't associate with the dear, and never with the undear. Not seeing those who are dear is painful, (as is) seeing those who are not dear.

3

211 Therefore let nothing be dear to you, for separation from the dear is (experienced as an) evil. There exist no bonds for those for whom there is neither the dear nor the undear.

4

212 From the dear arises grief; from the dear arises fear. For the one who is wholly free from the dear there exists no grief. Whence (should) fear (come)?

5

213 From affection (*pema*) arises grief; from affection arises fear. For one who is wholly free from affection there exists no grief. Whence (should) fear (come)?

6

214 From (sensual) enjoyment (*rati*) arises grief; from (sensual) enjoyment arises fear. For one who is wholly free from (sensual) enjoyment there is no grief. Whence (should) fear (come)?

7

215 From (lustful) desire (*kama*) arises grief; from (lustful) desire (*kama*) arises fear. For one who is

wholly free from (lustful) desire there is no grief.
Whence (should) fear (come)?

8

216 From craving arises grief; from craving arises
fear. For one who is wholly free from craving there
is no grief. Whence (should) fear (come)?

9

217 People hold him dear who is perfect in right
conduct (*sīla*) and vision (*dassana*), who is principled
(*dhammaṭṭha*) and a speaker of the truth, and who
carries out his own (spiritual) tasks.

10

218 He is called 'One whose stream goes upward'[11]
in whom is born an ardent aspiration (*chanda*) after
the Undefined, whose mind (*manasā*) would be
permeated (by the thrill of his progress so far), and
whose heart (*citta*) is unattached to sensual
pleasures.

11

219 When a man long absent (from home) returns
safely from a distant place, his relatives, friends, and
well-wishers rejoice exceedingly at his return.

12

220 Similarly, his own good deeds receive him when
he goes from this world to the other (world) as
relatives (receive) a dear one on his return (home).

XVII

ANGER

1

221 Let one give up anger, renounce conceit, (and) overcome all fetters. Suffering does not befall him who is unattached to name-and-form (*nāmarūpa*: i.e., psychophysical existence), (and) who is without (material or mental) possessions (*akiñcana*).

2

222 I call him a charioteer who holds back the arisen anger as though (holding back) a swerving chariot. Others are only holders of reins.

3

223 Overcome the angry by non-anger; overcome
the wicked with good. Overcome the miserly by
giving, the teller of lies with truth.

4

224 Speak the truth; do not get angry; give your
mite to those who ask (for alms). On these three
grounds one goes into the presence of the gods.

5

225 Those silent sages who are harmless
(*ahiṃsaka-s*) and always (self-)controlled go to the
Immoveable Abode, whither having gone they do
not grieve.

6

226 They come to the end of (their) defilements
(*āsava-s*), those who keep awake, who study day and
night, (and) who are intent on Nirvāṇa.

7

227 This is an old story, Atula,[12] not just one of
today. They blame him who is taciturn; they blame
him who is talkative; they even blame him who

speaks in moderation. There is no one in the world who is not blamed.

8

228 There has not been, nor will there be, nor is there anyone now, who is absolutely blamed or absolutely praised.

9–10

229–230 Who is entitled to blame that man who is like (a coin of) Jambunada gold,[13] a man who is praised by the wise, by those who have tested him day by day; one who is free from faults, a man of understanding, (and) whose wisdom and understanding are (well) integrated? Even the gods praise such a man. By Brahmā, too, is he praised.

11

231 Be on your guard against bodily agitation; be controlled in body. Giving up bodily misconduct, live well behaved as regards the body.

12

232 Be on your guard against verbal agitation; be controlled in speech. Giving up verbal misconduct, live well behaved as regards speech.

13

233 Be on your guard against mental agitation; be
controlled in mind. Giving up mental misconduct,
live well behaved as regards the mind.

14

234 They are the perfectly restrained ones, the wise
who are controlled in body and speech, (together
with) the wise who are controlled as regards the
mind.

XVIII

STAINS

I

235 You are now like a withered leaf; Death's men have approached you. You stand at the door of departure, and you do not even have provisions for the road.

2

236 Make a lamp (or: island) for yourself; strive quickly, (and) become one who is spiritually mature. With stains removed, (and) free from blemish, you will reach the celestial plane (*bhūmi*) of the spiritually developed (*ariya-s*).

3

237 You are now of advanced age; you have gone forth into the presence of Death. There is no (resting) place for you in between, (and) you do not even have provisions for the road.

4

238 Make a lamp (or: island) for yourself; strive quickly, (and) become one who is spiritually mature. With stains removed, (and) free from blemish, you will not undergo repeated birth and old age (any more).

5

239 The man of understanding removes his stains gradually, little by little, and from moment to moment, just as the silversmith (removes) the impurities of silver.

6

240 Just as rust springing from iron, (having) sprung from that eats it (away), even so his own actions lead the transgressor to an evil state (*duggati*).

7

241 Non-repetition is the stain of the (orally transmitted) sacred verses (*manta-s*). Inactivity (in maintaining them) is the stain of houses. Sloth is the stain of beauty (of complexion). Heedlessness is the stain of one who guards.

8

242 Misconduct is the stain of a woman. Stinginess is the stain of one who gives. (Both) in this world and the other (world) stains are indeed evil things.

9

243 A greater stain than these is ignorance (*avijjā*), which is the supreme stain. Abandoning this stain, be stainless, almsmen.

10

244 He has an easy life who is shameless, impudent as a crow, disparaging (of others' merits), obtrusive, arrogant, (and) of a corrupt way of life.

11

245 Life is hard for one with a sense of shame, who always seeks purity, who is unattached (or:

strenuous), who is humble (and) of a pure way of
life, and discerning.

12

246 Whoever in (this) world (of ours) destroys life,
tells lies, takes what is not given, resorts to the wives
of others,

13

247 and is addicted to the drinking of intoxicants
(*surāmeraya*), that man in this world himself digs up
his own roots (of merit).

14

248 Know this, good man: Those having an evil
nature are uncontrolled. Don't let greed and
unrighteousness subject you to prolonged suffering.

15

249 People give (alms) according to their faith and
at their good pleasure. One who is discontented
about the food and drink of others does not attain
concentration (*samādhi*), be it by day or by night.

16

250 One in whom this (kind of attitude) is extirpated, (it being) destroyed at its roots (and) abolished, he attains concentration (*samādhi*), be it by day or by night.

17

251 There is no fire like lust. There is no grip like anger. There is no net like delusion. There is no river like craving.

18

252 The faults of others are easily seen; one's own faults are seen with difficulty. One winnows the faults of others like chaff, but one covers up one's own as a dishonest gambler (covers up) a losing throw (of the dice).

19

253 He who pays attention to the faults of others (and) is always irritable, his defilements (*āsava-s*) grow. He is far from the destruction of the defilements.

20

254 There is no track in the sky. There is no (true) asketic outside (this Teaching). The race of men delight in illusion (*papañca*). The Tathāgatās (i.e., the Buddhas or Enlightened Ones) are free from illusions.

21

255 There is no track in the sky. There is no (true) asketic outside (this Teaching). There are no conditioned things that are eternal. There is no vacillation in the Enlightened Ones.

XIX

THE MAN OF PRINCIPLE

1

256 He is not a 'man of principle' (*dhammaṭṭha*) who rashly judges what is advantageous (*attha*). The spiritually mature person who judges both what is advantageous and disadvantageous –

2

257 who judges others impartially, carefully, and in accordance with principle – that man of understanding, guarded of principle, is said to be 'a man of principle'.

3

258 A man is not spiritually mature (or: learned) merely because he talks a lot. He is said to be spiritually mature who is secure (in himself), friendly, and without fear.

4

259 He is not a vessel of the Teaching (*dhammadhara*) merely because he talks a lot. He who, having heard only a little, personally sees the Truth, he (truly) is a 'vessel of the Teaching', that man who is not neglectful of the Teaching.

5

260 A man is not an elder (among almsmen) because his head is grey. Though of mature age, he is called 'grown old in vain'.

6

261 He is (truly) called an elder (among almsmen) in whom are truth and principle, (together with) harmlessness (*ahiṃsā*), (self-)control (and) restraint, (and) who is without stain and wise.

7

262 One who is jealous, miserly, and dishonest is not accounted 'good' (*sādhurūpa*) merely by reason of his speechifying or beautiful complexion.

8

263 He is said to be 'good' (*sādhurūpa*), that fault-free man of understanding, in whom this (kind of behaviour) is extirpated, it being destroyed at its roots (and) abolished.

9

264 A man who is without (religious) observances (and) who speaks what is false is not an asketic (merely) by reason of his shaven head.

10

265 He who stills (*sameti*) all his evils, small and great, is said to be an asketic (*samana*) because those evils have been stilled.

11

266 One is not an almsman (merely) because he begs (alms) from others. One is not an almsman (merely) because of having adopted a bad (teaching).

12

267 He is said to be an almsman who lives in the
world with discrimination (*saṅkhā*), having by means
of the spiritual life (*brahmacariya*) set aside merit and
demerit.

13–14

268–269 One who is confused and ignorant does not
become a silent sage (*munī*) merely by observing
silence. But that spiritually mature person who, as if
holding a pair of scales, accepts the best and rejects
the evil, *he* is a silent sage. He is a silent sage for that
(very) reason. He is (also) called a silent sage (*munī*)
because he understands (*munāti*) both worlds.

15

270 A man who harms living beings is not one who
is spiritually developed (*ariya*). He is said to be
spiritually developed who is harmless towards all
living beings.

16–17

271–272 Without having attained to the destruction
of the defilements (*asava-s*), almsman, you should
not rest content with rules of conduct and religious

observances, or with much learning, with the attainment of concentration (*samādhi*), or with living in seclusion, nor with (thinking) 'I enjoy the bliss of renunciation (that is) unknown to ordinary people.'

XX

THE WAY

1

273 Best of ways is the Eightfold (Way). Best of truths are the Four (Truths). Passionlessness is the best of (mental) states. The Man of Vision (*cakkhumā*) is the best of bipeds.

2

274 This indeed is the Way; there is no other that leads to purity of vision. Enter upon the Way; this Way is the bewilderment of Māra.

3

275 Following this Way you will make an end of
suffering. This indeed is the Way proclaimed by me
ever since I knew how to draw out the darts (of
craving).

4

276 By you must the zealous effort be made. The
Tathāgatās (i.e. Buddhas or Enlightened Ones)
are only proclaimers (of the Way). Those who are
practitioners, absorbed (in higher meditative states)
(eventually) win release from the bondage of Māra.

5

277 'All conditioned things are impermanent.' When
one sees this with insight (*pannā*) one becomes
weary of suffering. This is the Way to Purity.

6

278 'All conditioned things are painful.' When one
sees this with insight (*pannā*) one becomes weary of
suffering. This is the Way to Purity.

7

279 'All things (whatsoever) are devoid of unchanging selfhood.' When one sees this with insight (*pannā*) one becomes weary of suffering. This is the Way to Purity.

8

280 One who does not make use of his (spiritual) opportunities, who, though young and strong, is lazy, weak in aspiration, and inactive, such a lazy person does not find the way to insight (*pannā*).

9

281 Guarded in speech, as well as controlled in mind, let one do no (ethically) unskilful thing with the body. Purifying these three avenues of action, let him attain the Way made known by the sages.

10

282 From application (*yogā*) arises the (spiritually) great (*bhūri*). From lack of application the (spiritually) great wanes. Having known these two avenues of increase and decrease (of the great) let him so establish himself that the great may flourish.

11

283 Cut down the (whole) forest, not (just) one
tree. From the forest arises fear. Cutting down both
wood and brushwood, be 'out of the wood',
almsman.

12

284 To the extent that one has not cut down the last
little bit of this 'brushwood' of (the craving of) man
for woman, to that extent his mind will be fettered,
as the sucking calf to its mother.

13

285 Cut off your sticky affection, as one plucks with
one's hand the white autumnal lotus. Develop the
Way of Peace, the Nirvāṇa taught by the Happy
One.

14

286 'Here shall I stay during the rains, here in the
cold season and the hot.' Thus thinks the spiritually
immature person. He does not understand the
dangers (to life).

15

287 That infatuated man whose delight is in offspring and cattle, death goes and carries him off as a great flood (sweeps away) a sleeping village.

16

288 Sons are no protection, nor father, nor yet (other) relatives. For him who is seized by the End-maker (i.e., Death), there is no protection forthcoming from relatives.

17

289 Knowing the significance of this, let the spiritually mature person, the man restrained by good conduct, speedily cleanse the Way leading to Nirvāṇa.

XXI

THE MISCELLANEOUS

I

290 If by renouncing a limited happiness one would see an abundant happiness, let the spiritually mature person, having regard to the abundant happiness, sacrifice the limited happiness.

2

291 He who, contaminated by (his) association with hatred, seeks happiness for himself by inflicting suffering on others, is not released from hatred.

3

292 What is to be done, that is neglected; what is
not to be done, that is done. Of those who are
arrogant and heedless the defilements increase.

4

293 Those who ever earnestly practise mindfulness
with regard to the body, not following after what is
not to be done (and) steadfastly pursuing what is to
be done, of these mindful and fully attentive ones
the defilements come to an end.

5

294 Having slain mother and father and two warrior
kings, and having destroyed a kingdom together
with the (king's) revenue collector, the brāhmaṇa
goes free from sin.[14]

6

295 Having slain mother and father and two learned
kings, and having killed a tiger as the fifth, the
brāhmaṇa goes free from sin.[15]

7

296 Wide awake they always arise (in the morning),
the disciples of Gotama, (those) who day and night

are constantly mindful of the (virtues of the)
Buddha.

8

297 Wide awake they always arise (in the morning),
the disciples of Gotama, (those) who day and night
are constantly mindful of the (qualities of the)
Dhamma.

9

298 Wide awake they always arise (in the morning),
the disciples of Gotama, (those) who day and night
are constantly mindful of the (characteristics of the
Ārya) Sangha.[16]

10

299 Wide awake they always arise (in the morning),
the disciples of Gotama, (those) who day and night
are constantly mindful of the (transitory nature of
the) body.

11

300 Wide awake they always arise (in the morning),
the disciples of Gotama, (those) who day and night
delight in non-injury (*ahiṃsā*).

12

301 Wide awake they always arise (in the morning), the disciples of Gotama, (those) whose mind day and night delights in meditation (*bhāvanā*).

13

302 It is difficult to go forth (from home to the homeless life); and difficult to delight therein (once one has gone forth). (At the same time) household life is painful, (and) painful, likewise, is living together with those who are not (one's) peers. Travellers (on the road of birth, death, and rebirth) are oppressed by suffering, so do not be (such a) traveller oppressed by suffering.

14

303 He who is perfect in faith and good conduct, (and) possessed of fame and wealth, he is honoured everywhere, to whatever country he resorts.

15

304 Like the Snowy (Mountain Range), the good are visible even from afar. The wicked are not seen, like arrows shot in the night.

16

305 He who sits alone, lies down alone (and) walks alone, without weariness, (and) who strives, (all) alone, to subdue himself, (he) will take delight in the (solitude of the) forest.

XXII

THE WOEFUL STATE

I

306 One who tells lies arises (by way of rebirth) in
a state of woe, as does one who, having done
something, says 'I don't do (that sort of thing).'
These two sons of Manu (the Primeval
Progenitor),[17] men of base actions, on departing
(this life) have the same (painful destiny) in the
other world.

2

307 Many 'yellow-necks' (i.e., wearers of the yellow
robe)[18] are of bad qualities (or: of an evil disposition)

and uncontrolled. These bad people, on account of their bad deeds, arise (after death) in a state of woe.

3

308   Better to swallow a flaming, red hot ball of iron, than to be an immoral, uncontrolled man living on the almsfood of the land.

4

309   A heedless man who resorts to the wives of others comes by four (evil) states: acquisition of demerit; not sleeping (soundly) as desired; thirdly, blame; (and) fourthly, (rebirth in) a state of woe.

5

310   (The result is) acquisition of demerit and a wretched (future) course; the short-lived enjoyment of an apprehensive man with an apprehensive woman; also the king imposes a heavy penalty. Therefore let not a man resort to another's wife.

6

311   Just as (sharp-edged) kusa grass, wrongly taken hold of, cuts the hand, so the life of a religieux, wrongly grasped, drags down to a state of woe.

7

312 Any unprincipled act, and any sullied religious observance – a (slack) spiritual life (*brahmacariya*) filled with suspicion – this is of little benefit.

8

313 If you have something to do, attack it vigorously. One who lives the homeless life half-heartedly scatters much dust of passion around.

9

314 An ill deed is better left undone, (for) an ill deed torments one afterwards (with remorse). Better done is a good deed, having done which one is not (so) tormented.

10

315 Like a frontier city well-guarded within and without, so guard yourself. Let not the (fortunate) moment (of human birth etc.) pass you by. Those who allow the fortunate moment to pass by grieve when they go to the woeful state.

11

316 Those who are ashamed of what is not shameful, (and) not ashamed of what is shameful,

such beings, taking upon themselves wrong views, go to an evil state.

12

317 Those who see what (morally) is not fearful as fearful, and who see what (morally) is fearful as not fearful, such beings, taking upon themselves wrong views, go to an evil state.

13

318 Those who think what (morally) is blameable not blameable, and who see what (morally) is not blameable as blameable, such beings, taking upon themselves wrong views, go to an evil state.

14

319 Knowing the (morally) blameable as blameable, and the (morally) free from blame as blameless, those beings, taking upon themselves right views, go to a happy state.

XXIII

THE ELEPHANT

1

320 I shall patiently endure abuse, just as the (trained) elephant endures in battle the arrow (shot) from a bow. The many are indeed ill-natured (or: badly behaved).

2

321 The tamed (elephant) is led to the assembly; the king mounts the tamed (elephant). Among men, best is the (self-)controlled person who patiently endures abuse.

3

322 Trained mules are best, also (equine)
thoroughbreds of Sindh, and the mighty (fighting)
elephants. (But) best of all is the self-controlled
man.

4

323 One does not go to the unfrequented realm by
such vehicles as these, as does a controlled one go
(to it) by means of a well-subdued, disciplined self.

5

324 The elephant called Dhanapāla is difficult to
restrain when his temples are streaming with must
(in the time of rut). Shackled, he refuses (his) food.
The tusker remembers the (delightful) elephant
forest.

6

325 When one is sluggish and gluttonous, given to
sleep, (and) a roller-about like a great hog fed on
grains, such a stupid person goes again and again to
a womb (to be reborn).

7

326 Formerly this mind (of mine) went wandering about where it wished, as it liked, (and) according to its pleasure. Today I will control it radically, as the wielder of the (elephant driver's) hook restrains the (rutting) elephant.

8

327 Be delighters in non-heedlessness. Keep watch over your mind. Lift yourself clear of the difficult road (of the mental defilements), as an elephant sunk in a bog (hauls himself out).

9

328 Should you get a sensible companion, one who is fit company (for you), who behaves well, and is wise, (then) go about with him joyous and mindful, overcoming all (external and internal) dangers.

10

329 Should you not get a sensible companion, one who is fit company (for you), who behaves well, and is wise, (then) go about alone, like a king forsaking a conquered country, (or) like an elephant (living solitary) in the Mātaṅga forest.

11

330 It is better to go about alone; there is no companionship with the spiritually immature. Going about alone one commits no sins, like an elephant living unconcerned in the Mātaṅga forest.

12

331 Friends are good in time of need. Contentment is good in every way. At the end of life (a store of) merit is good (or: a meritorious action is good). Good is the leaving behind of all suffering.

13

332 Here reverence for mother is good; reverence for father is also good. Here reverence for asketicism is good; reverence for holiness is also good.

14

333 The lifelong practice of virtue (*sīla*) is good. A (firmly) established faith (in the Three Jewels) is good. Good is the getting of wisdom (*paññā*). The non-doing of evil is good.

XXIV

CRAVING

1

334 The craving of the man who lives carelessly increases like the māluvā creeper. He runs from existence to existence, like a monkey in the jungle (leaping from tree to tree) in search of fruit.

2

335 Whoever in the world is overcome by this wretched, adhesive craving, his sorrows grows like the bīraṇa grass that is rained upon.

3

336 Whoever in the world overcomes this wretched, adhesive craving, so difficult to overcome, his sorrows fall from him like drops of water from the lotus leaf.

4

337 I tell you this: Be of good cheer, as many of you as are here assembled. Dig out the root of craving, as the seeker of the usīra (digs out) the bīraṇa grass. Don't let Māra (the Evil One) break you again and again as a river (in spate) breaks the reed.

5

338 Just as a felled tree shoots (up) again if the root is uninjured and stout, so this suffering (of ours) arises again and again if the propensity to craving is not destroyed.

6

339 The currents of his passion-based thoughts carry him away, that man of wrong views for whom the thirty-six streams (of craving)[19] flowing towards what is pleasurable are strong.

7

340 The streams (of craving) flow everywhere, (and) the creeper (of craving) having sprung up remains (clasping its objects). Seeing that creeper sprung up, sever its root with (the knife of) wisdom (*paññā*).

8

341 Delights arise for a being, (delights) that rush on and are saturated (with craving). Those seekers after pleasure who are attached to what is agreeable, those men are indeed bound for (re)birth and old age.

9

342 Attended upon by craving, the race of men run about in terror like a trapped hare. Fettered and bound (as they are), suffering befalls them again and again for a long time.

10

343 Attended upon by craving, the race of men run about in terror like a trapped hare. Therefore let him allay craving, the almsman who is desirous of his own freedom from passion.

11

344 Just look at him, the man who having been
delivered from the jungle of craving (i.e., from the
household life) and drawn to (the life of) the jungle,
(nonetheless) having been thus delivered from the
jungle (of craving) runs (from the jungle) to the
jungle (of household life). Freed, he runs (back) to
(his former) bondage.

12

345 That is not a strong bond, say the wise, which is
made of iron, wood, or (plaited) grass. Passionate
fondness for jewelled earrings, (and) longing with
regard to sons and wives –

13

346 that is a strong bond, say the wise. It drags one
down, is loose (fitting) yet difficult to be got rid of.
This (bond) they too cut off, those longing-free ones
who, giving up sensual pleasures, go forth (from the
household life).

14

347 The passionately lustful man falls back into the
torrent (of repeated existence), just as the spider
returns to (the centre of) its web (after running out

and feeding on a trapped fly). This too the wise man cuts off and renounces; free from longing, he leaves behind all suffering.

15
348 Give up what is 'before' (in time), give up what is 'after', give up what is 'in between'. Crossed to the Further Shore of existence, (and) with mind wholly released, you will undergo birth and decay no more.

16
349 For the person of disturbed thinking, whose passions are acute, and who looks (only) for what is 'lovely', craving grows apace.

17
350 He who delights in calming down (his) thinking, who meditates on the ('lovely' as being truly) unlovely, (and) who is always mindful, he will cut through the bond of Māra (the Evil One).

18
351 The one who has arrived at (spiritual) perfection, who is devoid of fear, free from craving, and without (moral) blemish, (that person) has

wrenched out the darts of (mundane) existence.
This is the last body (he will wear).

19

352 One who is free from craving, not grasping,
skilled in the explanation of (doctrinal) terms, and
who would understand the words (of the Buddha's
Teaching) in context, that person is truly called 'a
wearer of his last body', 'very wise', (and) 'a great
man'.

20

353 I am all-conquering, all-knowing, (and) unattached
to all things. All abandoning, freed through the
destruction of craving, (and) having by myself
thoroughly comprehended (the destruction of
craving), whom should I point out (as my teacher)?[20]

21

354 The gift of the Dhamma surpasses all gifts. The
taste of the Dhamma surpasses all tastes. Delight in
the Dhamma surpasses all delights. The destruction
of craving overcomes all suffering.

22

355 Possessions strike (down) the man of evil understanding, but not those who are seekers of the Beyond. Because of his craving for possessions, the man of evil understanding strikes himself (down) as if he were striking (down) others.

23

356 Weeds are the blemish of (cultivated) fields, lust of this (human) race. Hence what is given to those free from lust is productive of much fruit (in the shape of merit).

24

357 Weeds are the blemish of (cultivated) fields, hatred of this (human) race. Hence what is given to those free from hate is productive of much fruit (in the shape of merit).

25

358 Weeds are the blemish of (cultivated) fields, delusion of this (human) race. Hence what is given to those free from delusion is productive of much fruit (in the shape of merit).

26

359 Weeds are the blemish of (cultivated) fields, covetousness of this (human) race. Hence what is given to those free from covetousness is productive of much fruit (in the shape of merit).

XXV

THE ALMSMAN

1

360 Restraint with the eye is good; good is restraint by the ear; restraint by the nose is good; good is restraint with the tongue.

2

361 Bodily restraint is good; good is restraint in speech; restraint of the mind is good; good in all respects is restraint. The almsman who is in all respects restrained is freed from all suffering.

3

362 He is truly called an almsman whose hands are controlled, whose feet are controlled, whose speech is controlled, who is controlled in thought (or: supremely controlled), whose delight is within, (and) who is collected, solitary, content.

4

363 The utterance is sweet of that almsman who controls his mouth, who speaks in moderation, who is not puffed up (with his knowledge), (and) who explains the meaning (of the Buddha's words) and their practical application.

5

364 An almsman who abides in the Teaching, who delights in the Teaching, who reflects on the Teaching, and who bears the Teaching in mind, will not fall away from the True Teaching (*saddhamma*).

6

365 Let one not despise what he has gained (by way of alms); let him not live envying the gains of others. The almsman who envies the gains of others does not attain to (meditative) concentration.

7

366 Even if an almsman's gains (by way of alms) be very little, let him not despise what he has gained. The gods praise him who is of pure livelihood (and) unwearied.

8

367 He is indeed called an almsman for whom nowhere in the mind and body is there anything of which to say 'This is mine,' and who does not grieve for what does not (really) exist.

9

368 The almsman who dwells in loving-kindness, (and) who is happy in the mandate of the Buddha, would attain to the state that is peace (i.e., Nirvāṇa), to the quieting of conditioned existence (and) to bliss.

10

369 Almsman, empty this boat! Emptied, it will go more (quickly and) lightly for you. Having cut out lust and hatred, you will then go to Nirvāṇa.

11

370   Cut away five, abandon five, (and) in addition
cultivate five. The almsman who has transcended
the five attachments is called 'One who has crossed
the flood'.[21]

12

371   Be absorbed (in higher meditative states),
almsman! Don't be heedless. Don't allow your mind
to whirl about among sensual pleasures. Don't
through heedlessness swallow a (red hot) iron ball,
(and then) when it scorches you cry out 'What
torment!'

13

372   There is no absorption in higher meditative
states (*jhāna*) for one who is without wisdom
(*paññā*); there is no wisdom for one who is
unabsorbed in higher meditative states. He in whom
are found (both) absorption in higher mental states
and wisdom is truly in the (very) presence of
Nirvāṇa.

14

373   For the almsman who enters an empty cottage,
who is of peaceful mind, and who perfectly

comprehends the Dharma, there is a joy surpassing that of men.

15

374 Howsoever one grasps (the fact of) the rise and fall of the aggregates (of conditioned existence), he attains a joy and delight that, to the discerning person, is (as) nectar.

16

375 Here (in the world) the first thing for the wise almsman is this: control of the senses, contentment, restraint through observance of the (almsman's) code of conduct, and association with friends who are virtuous, of pure life, (and) energetic.

17

376 Let one be hospitable (and) well-mannered. Being on this account full of happiness one will make an end of suffering.

18

377 Just as the jasmine (creeper) sheds its withered flowers so, almsmen, should you totally get rid of lust and hatred.

19

378 He who is tranquil in body, tranquil in speech, (and) possessed of (mental) tranquillity, who is well integrated, (and) who has left behind worldly things – such an almsman is said to be at peace.

20

379 Yourself reprove yourself. Yourself examine yourself. Thus self-guarded (and) mindful the almsman will live happily.

21

380 One is one's own protector; what other protector should there be? Therefore control this self of yours as a trader (manages) a noble steed.

22

381 The almsman who is full of joy (and) happy in the instruction of the Buddha will attain to the State of Peace, to the blissful allaying of (mundane) conditions.

23

382 A youthful almsman, even, who commits himself to the Buddha's instruction, lights up the world like the moon (when) freed from cloud.

XXVI

THE BRĀHMAŅA

1

383 Exert yourself and cut off the stream;[22] do away with sense-desires, brāhmaṇa. Having known the destruction of mundane conditionings, be a Knower of the Unmade, brāhmaṇa.

2

384 When the brāhmaṇa has 'crossed over' in respect of the two states, (i.e., calm and insight), then all the fetters of that knowing one come to an end.

3

385 I call him a brāhmaṇa for whom there exists neither the Further Shore nor the hither shore, nor both, (and) who is without distress and free from (all) bonds.

4

386 I call him a brāhmaṇa who is absorbed (in higher meditative states), who is unstained (by passion), whose task is done, who is free from the defilements (or: unbiased), (and) who has reached the Ultimate Goal.

5

387 The sun shines bright by day; the moon shines at night; the armed warrior shines bright; the brāhmaṇa who is absorbed (in higher meditative states) shines bright. But the Buddha shines bright by day and by night, (shining) with splendour.

6

388 'Brāhmaṇa' means one who 'bars out' evil; he is said to be an asketic (samaṇa) who lives in quiet (sama); he is said to be a 'goer forth' (from the household life) who has 'sent forth into banishment' his own impurities.[23]

7

389 One should not strike a brāhmaṇa, nor should
the brāhmaṇa (who is struck) give vent (to anger).
Shame on (or: woe to) him who strikes a brāhmaṇa!
More shame on (or: woe to) him who gives vent (to
anger).

8

390 For a brāhmaṇa there is nothing better than a
mind restrained from (its) likings. To the extent that
the harming mind turns back (from harming), to
that extent suffering is stopped.

9

391 I call him a brāhmaṇa by whom no evil is done
by the body, by speech, (or) by the mind, and who
with regard to these three is restrained.

10

392 As a brahmin worships the sacrificial fire, so let
one pay homage to the person from whom one
comes to know the Truth (*dhamma*) taught by the
Perfectly Enlightened One.

11

393 One is not a brāhmaṇa on account of matted hair, or (one's) clan, or birth. He in whom there exists both truth and principle (*dhamma*), *he* is pure, *he* is a brāhmaṇa.

12

394 What use (your) matted hair, (you) man of evil understanding; what use your deerskin garment? Within, you are a dense jungle (of passions), (yet) you touch up the outside.

13

395 The man who wears rags from a dust heap, who is lean, whose veins stand out all over the body, (and) who, alone and in the forest, is absorbed (in higher meditative states), *him* I call a brāhmaṇa.

14

396 I do not call him a brāhmaṇa who is (merely) womb-born or sprung from a (brahmin) mother. If he is a man of possessions (*sakiñcana*) he is (simply) called 'one who addresses others familiarly'. I call him a brāhmaṇa who is free from attachment and without possessions (*akiñcana*).

15

397 I call him a brāhmaṇa who, having severed all bonds, does not tremble, and who has unburdened himself of all attachments.

16

398 I call him a brāhmaṇa who has severed the bond (of hatred), the thong (of craving), and the cord (of wrong views) together with its concomitants, who has lifted the crossbar (of ignorance), (and) who is Enlightened.

17

399 I call him a brāhmaṇa who, being good, patiently endures abuse, flogging, and imprisonment, and whose strong army is the strength of patience.

18

400 I call him a brāhmaṇa who is without anger, who (scrupulously) observes (religious) vows, who is ethical, free from lust, (and) controlled, (and) who wears his last body.

19

401 I call him a brāhmaṇa who, like (a drop of) water on a lotus leaf, or a mustard seed on the point of an awl, does not cling to (lit., is not smeared with) sensuous pleasures.

20

402 I call him a brāhmaṇa who in this very life has personally known the destruction of suffering, who has laid down the burden (of conditioned existence), (and) who is detached (from the world).

21

403 I call him a brāhmaṇa whose knowledge is deep, who is a man of understanding, who knows what is and what is not the Way, (and) who has reached the Supreme Goal.

22

404 I call him a brāhmaṇa who socializes with neither householders nor homeless ones (anāgārika-s), who lives free from attachment (lit., lives houseless), (and) who desires little or nothing.

23

405 I call him a brāhmaṇa who has abandoned violence towards living beings, be they moving about or stationary (or: whether trembling and afraid or firm-minded), and who neither slays nor causes (others) to slay.

24

406 I call him a brāhmaṇa who is conciliatory among the antagonistic, peaceful among those who have recourse to violence (*daṇḍa*), (and) who is unattached among the attached.

25

407 I call him a brāhmaṇa from whom lust, hatred, pride, and hypocrisy have fallen away like a mustard seed from the point of an awl.

26

408 I call him a brāhmaṇa who would utter gentle, instructive, true speech by which one would give offence to no one.

27

409 I call him a brāhmaṇa who takes, in this world, nothing that is not given (to him), be it long or short, small or great, pleasant or unpleasant.

28

410 I call him a brāhmaṇa in whom are found no longings either for this world or the other (world), who is (utterly) free from longings (and) who is released from all defilements.

29

411 I call him a brāhmaṇa who, through perfect knowledge, is free from doubts, (and) who has achieved the plunge into the Deathless (*amata*).

30

412 I call him a brāhmaṇa who here (in this world) has transcended good and bad, together with attachment, and who is free from sorrow, without passion, (and) pure.

31

413 I call him a brāhmaṇa who is spotless and pure as the moon, clear(-minded) and undisturbed (by

the defilements), and in whom delight (in
conditioned existence) has been extinguished.

32

414 I call him a brāhmaṇa who has passed over this
dangerous (or: muddy) track (of the passions), this
fortress of delusion that is repeated existence, who
has crossed (the flood) and reached the Further
Shore, who is absorbed (in higher meditative states),
who is passionless and free from doubts, (and) who,
being without (further) clinging, is at peace (in
Nirvāṇa).

33

415 I call him a brāhmaṇa who, having here (in the
world) given up the pleasures of sense, goes forth as
a homeless one, and who has destroyed (craving for)
sensuous existence.

34

416 I call him a brāhmaṇa who, having here (in the
world) given up craving, goes forth as a homeless
one, and who has destroyed craving for
(conditioned) existence.

35

417 I call him a brāhmaṇa who, having discarded human bonds and transcended celestial bonds, is delivered from all bonds (whatsoever).[24]

36

418 I call him a brāhmaṇa who has given up attachment and aversion, become tranquil (lit., cool), (and) free from the substrates (of conditioned existence), (and who thus is) a hero victorious over the whole world.

37

419 I call him a brāhmaṇa who knows, in every way, the passing away and arising of living beings, who is unattached, living happily, and Enlightened.

38

420 I call him a brāhmaṇa whose track gods, celestial musicians,[25] and human beings do not know, that (supremely) worthy one who has destroyed the defilements.

39

421 I call him a brāhmaṇa for whom there is nothing before, or after, or in between, who is

without (material or mental) possessions, (and) who
is unattached.

40

422 I call him a brāhmaṇa who is foremost (among
men), excellent, heroic, a great sage, the victorious
one, the one who is passionless, washed (clean of
the defilements), (and) Enlightened.

41

423 I call him a brāhmaṇa who knows his previous
lives (lit., abodes), who sees heaven and the state of
woe, who has reached the extinction of births, who
is a silent sage, a master of the higher knowledge
(*abhiññā*), (and) who has accomplished all that is to
be accomplished.

NOTES

1   In Buddhist mythology, Māra is the ruler of the realm of sense desire (*kāmaloka*) as Brahmā is the ruler of the realm of archetypal form (*rūpaloka*). He is the Evil One (*pāpimā*), representing as he does the forces that obstruct the attainment of Enlightenment.

2   'Here' (*idha*) refers to this world and 'there' (*pecca*) to the next world.

3   A.P. Buddhadatta Maha Thera (*Dhammapadaṃ*: An Anthology of the Sayings of the Buddha, Colombo, n.d., p.6) comments: 'This is the only place in the Pāli where where this word [*sahitaṃ*] occurs to indicate "literature". It is doubtful whether this was used here to mean the same thing. Another possibility here is to take this as two words *sa* and *hitam* instead of one. If we take it as two words we have to translate it as:

"Though much he speaks about beneficial things".'

4 The Immortal or Deathless (*amata*) is a synonym for Nirvāṇa.

5 Like Cupid, Māra is thought of as carrying a bow and arrows, and his arrows are 'flower-tipped', the flowers being the pleasures of sense.

6 Kusa-grass was used in Vedic rituals, hence 'sacred'.

7 The Factors of Enlightenment (*bodhi-aṅga-s* or *bojjhaṅga-s*) are mindfulness (*sati*), investigation of mental states (*dhamma-vicaya*), energy (*viriya*), rapture (*pīti*), tranquillity (*passadhi*), concentration (*samādhi*), and equanimity (*upekkhā*).

8 According to tradition, these two verses were spoken by the Buddha immediately after his attainment of Enlightenment.

9 The 'path of the sun' (*ādiccapatha*) is the sky.

10 The gods of Brilliant Light (*abhassarā-deva-s*) in Buddhist mythology are a class of gods occupying in the celestial hierarchy a place immediately above the various Brahmās. Their subjective or 'psychological' counterpart is the second *jhāna* or 'absorption'.

11 'One whose stream goes upward' (*uddhaṃsuto*) is one the current of whose being is directed towards Nirvāṇa.

12 Atula was a layman who blamed various bhikkhus in the ways mentioned by the Buddha.

13 'Jambunada gold' is gold from the river of that name.

14 The 'mother' is craving (*taṇhā*), the 'father' self-conceit (*māna*), the 'two warrior kings' are the two wrong views of eternalism and annihilationism, the 'kingdom' comprises the twelve bases (*āyatana-s*), i.e., the six sense organs, including the mind, and their respective objects, while the 'revenue collector' (*sānucara*) is the passionate delight that arises in dependence on the twelve bases. Here 'Brāhmaṇa' is synonymous with Arahant.

15 The 'two learned kings' are the two wrong views of eternalism and annihilationism, the tiger is doubt (*vicikicchā*), which also happens to be the fifth hindrance (*nivāraṇa*).

16 Here the Sangha is the Ārya Sangha, consisting of those of the Buddha's disciples, past, present, and future, who are Stream-Entrants, Once-Returners, Non-Returners, and Arahants. To these the Mahāyāna would add the great Bodhisattvas.

17 Manu is the Primeval Progenitor of Vedic tradition, and a 'son of Manu' is therefore a human being (cf. the expression 'children of Adam').

18 A 'yellow-neck' (*kāsāvakaṇṭha*) is a wearer of the yellow robe of the almsman (*bhikkhu*).

19 The 'thirty-six streams (of craving)' are the three kinds of craving (*taṇhā*) – for sense pleasures, for existence, and for non-existence – multiplied by the six internal plus the six external bases (*āyatana-s*).

20 These are the words with which according to the
Ariyapariyesanā-sutta (*Majjhima-Nikāya* 26), the Buddha
responded when asked by a naked ascetic, shortly after
his Enlightenment, who was his teacher.

21 The five that are to be 'cut away' are the fetters
(*saṃyojana-s*) of self-view, doubt, dependence on
moral rules and religious observances, lust, and ill
will. These five bind one to the realm of sense-desire.
The five that are to be 'abandoned' are the fetters of
desire for existence in the realm of archetypal form,
desire for existence in the formless realm, conceit,
restlessness, and ignorance. These bind one to the
realm of archetypal form and the realm of
formlessness. The five that are to be 'cultivated' are
the five spiritual faculties (*indriya-s*) of faith, wisdom,
concentration, energy, and mindfulness.

22 The 'stream' (*sota*) is the process of repeated birth,
death, and rebirth.

23 In this verse there is a play upon words which I have
tried to reproduce.

24 Human bonds (*mānusaka-yoga-s*) are the desire for
continued existence, or rebirth, in the human realm;
'celestial bonds' (*dibba-yoga-s*) are the desire for rebirth
in the realm of the gods.

25 In Buddhist mythology 'celestial musicians'
(*gandhabba-s*) are a class of gods inhabiting the realm
of the Four Great Kings. They are so called because
they live on scent (*gandha*).

GLOSSARY

Aggregate: (Pāli, *khandha*) All phenomena are
  'compounded' or 'put together', and are therefore
  aggregates of other phenomena. Traditionally, these are
  divided into five types: form (*rūpa*), feeling (*vedanā*),
  perception (*saññā*), volition (*saṅkhāra*), and
  consciousness (*viññāna*).

Brahmā: The most powerful and longest lived of all the
  'gods', q.v.

Brāhmaṇa: See Note 15.

Conditioned existence: (*paṭiccasamuppāda*) Everything arises
  in dependence upon conditions, thus the mundane
  world is spoken of as conditioned existence.

Deathless: (*amata*) a synonym for Nirvāṇa (q.v.).

Defilements: (*āsava-s*) The biases toward sensuous experience (*kāma*), conditioned existence (*bhava*), speculative opinions (*diṭṭhi*), and ignorance (*avijja*).

Dhamma: The Truth; the teaching of the Buddha.

Eightfold Way: One way of describing the path leading to Enlightenment, consisting of Perfect Vision, Perfect Emotion, Perfect Speech, Perfect Action, Perfect Livelihood, Perfect Effort, Perfect Awareness, and Perfect Samādhi.

Empty: (*suñña*) Absolute reality is not 'conditioned' or 'compounded' of anything, and is therefore described as Empty.

Fetters: See Note 22.

Four (Ariyan) Truths: These are the fundamental truths of Buddhism: the existence of unsatisfactoriness (*dukkha*), craving (*taṇhā*) as its cause, its cessation (*nirvāṇa*), and the way leading to its cessation (the Eightfold Way, q.v.)

Further shore: (*pāra*) a synonym for Nirvāṇa (q.v.).

Gods: (*deva-s*) Beings that dwell on the higher, more blissful, planes of existence. See also Note 11.

Immoveable: (*accuta*) a synonym for Nirvāṇa (q.v.).

Noble Ones: (*ariya-s*) Those who have gained Enlightenment or are shortly to do so, consisting of Stream-Entrants (q.v.) (*sotāpanna-s*), Once-Returners (*sakadāgāmi-s*), Non-Returners (*anāgāmi-s*), and Enlightened beings (*arahant-s*).

Nirvāṇa: (Pāli *nibbāna*) lit., 'blowing out'; the
  extinguishing of all the fires of craving. Nirvāṇa or
  Enlightenment is the goal of all Buddhists.

Perfectly Awakened One: (*sammāsambuddha*) The Buddha.

Stream Entry: (*sotāpatti*) The point at which one has
  established transcendental insight such that one can no
  longer fall away from the path. Traditionally,
  Enlightenment will then be attained within a maximum
  of seven more lifetimes.

Supernormal powers: (*iddhi*) the powers and influence that
  emanate from a highly concentrated state of mental
  absorption.

Unmade: (*akaṭa*) That which is not compounded or
  conditioned, i.e., Nirvāṇa.

FURTHER READING

John Brough (ed.), *The Gāndhārī Dharmapada*, Oxford
   University Press, London 1962 (includes introduction
   and commentary)
Bhikkhu Kuala Lumpur Dhammajoti (trans.), *The Chinese
   Version of the Dharmapada*, University of Kelaniya, Sri
   Lanka 1995 (includes introduction and annotations)
K.R. Norman, *Pāli Literature*, Otto Harrassowitz,
   Wiesbaden 1983
K.R. Norman, *The Word of the Doctrine (Dhammapada)*, Pali
   Text Society, Oxford 1997
John Ross and Mahinda Palihawadana (trans.), *Buddhism:
   The Dhammapada* (Sacred Writings vol.6), Book-of-the-
   Month Club, New York 1992 (includes Pāli text)
Sangharakshita, *The Eternal Legacy*, Windhorse
   Publications, Birmingham 2006

Gareth Sparham, *The Tibetan Dharmapada*, Wisdom
Publications, London 1983 (a translation of the Tibetan
version of the *Udānavarga*)

WINDHORSE PUBLICATIONS

Windhorse Publications is a Buddhist charitable company based in the United Kingdom. We place great emphasis on producing books of high quality that are accessible and relevant to those interested in Buddhism at whatever level. We are the main publisher of the works of Sangharakshita, the founder of the Triratna Buddhist Order and Community. Our books draw on the whole range of the Buddhist tradition, including translations of traditional texts, commentaries, books that make links with contemporary culture and ways of life, biographies of Buddhists, and works on meditation.

As a not-for-profit enterprise, we ensure that all surplus income is invested in new books and improved production methods, to better communicate Buddhism in the twenty-first century. We welcome donations to help us continue our work – to find out more, go to windhorsepublications.com.

The Windhorse is a mythical animal that flies over the earth carrying on its back three precious jewels, bringing these invaluable gifts to all humanity: the Buddha (the 'Awakened One'), his teaching, and the community of all his followers.

Windhorse Publications	Consortium Book Sales	Windhorse Books
38 Newmarket Road	& Distribution	PO Box 574
Cambridge CB5 8DT	210 American Drive	Newtown NSW 2042
info@windhorsepublications.com	Jackson TN 38301	Australia
	USA	

THE TRIRATNA BUDDHIST COMMUNITY

Windhorse Publications is a part of the Triratna Buddhist Community, an international movement with centres in Europe, India, North and South America, and Australasia. At these centres, members of the Triratna Buddhist Order offer classes in meditation and Buddhism. Activities of the Triratna Community also include retreat centres, residential spiritual communities, ethical Right Livelihood businesses, and the Karuna Trust, a United Kingdom fundraising charity that supports social-welfare projects in the slums and villages of India.

Through these and other activities, Triratna is developing a unique approach to Buddhism, not simply as a philosophy and a set of techniques, but as a creatively directed way of life for all people living in the conditions of the modern world.

If you would like more information about Triratna please visit thebuddhistcentre. com or write to:

London Buddhist Centre	Aryaloka	Sydney Buddhist Centre
51 Roman Road	14 Heartwood Circle	24 Enmore Road
London E2 0HU	Newmarket NH 03857	Sydney NSW 2042
United Kingdom	USA	Australia

ALSO FROM WINDHORSE

BUDDHISM: TOOLS FOR LIVING YOUR LIFE
BY VAJRAGUPTA

Buddhism: Tools for Living Your Life is a guide for those seeking a meaningful spiritual path in busy – and often hectic – lives. An experienced teacher of Buddhism and meditation, Vajragupta provides clear explanations of the main Buddhist teachings, as well as a variety of exercises designed to help readers develop or deepen their practice.

ISBN 9781 899579 74 7
£12.99 / $17.95 / €15.95
192 pages

THE BUDDHA'S NOBLE EIGHTFOLD PATH
BY SANGHARAKSHITA

'Probably the best "life coaching" manual you'll ever read, the key to living with clarity and awareness.' Karen Robinson, *The Sunday Times*

The Noble Eightfold Path is the most widely known of the Buddha's teachings. It is ancient, extending back to the Buddha's first discourse and is highly valued as a unique treasury of wisdom and practical guidance on how to live our lives.

This introduction takes the reader deeper while always remaining practical, inspiring and accessible. Sangharakshita translates ancient teachings and makes them relevant to the way we live our lives today.

ISBN 9781 899579 81 5
£9.99 / $13.95 / €12.95
176 pages

SATIPATTHANA

THE DIRECT PATH TO REALIZATION

BY ANALAYO

This best-selling book offers a unique and detailed textual study of the *Satipatthana Sutta*, a foundational Buddhist discourse on meditation practice.

'...a gem... I learned a lot from this wonderful book and highly recommend it.' Joseph Goldstein

'An indispensible guide ... surely destined to become the classic commentary on the Satipatthana.' Christopher Titmuss

'This book should prove to be of value both to scholars of Early Buddhism and to serious meditators alike.' Bhikkhu Bodhi

'Very impressive and useful, with its blend of strong scholarship and attunement to practice issues.' Prof. Peter Harvey, author of *An Introduction to Buddhist Ethics*

ISBN 9781 899579 54 9
£17.99 / $27.95 / €19.95
336 pages

THE ART OF REFLECTION

BY RATNAGUNA

It is all too easy either to think obsessively, or to not think enough. But how do we think usefully? How do we reflect? Like any art, reflection can be learnt and developed, leading to a deeper understanding of life and to the fullness of wisdom.

The Art of Reflection is a practical guide to reflection as a spiritual practice, about 'what we think and how we think about it'. It is a book about contemplation and insight, and reflection as a way to discover the truth.

'This is a gem of a book that can be savoured and will enlighten.' Professor Paul Gilbert, author of *The Compassionate Mind*

'No-one who takes seriously the study and practice of the Dharma should fail to read this ground-breaking book.' Sangharakshita, founder of the Triratna Buddhist Community.

ISBN 9781 899579 89 1
£9.99 / $16.95 / €12.95
160 pages